Innervoice

Reflections

Sravan Kumar

BookLeaf
Publishing

India | USA | UK

Made with ❤ on the BookLeaf Publishing Platform
www.bookleafpub.in
www.bookleafpub.com

To all the readers who want to relax and enjoy reading poems dealing with themes and emotions like Love, Hatred, Anger, Pain, Hope, Ego, Jealousy and Peace, among others, I need not talk about the effect poetry has on the human mind. Still, at the same time, I would like to reiterate how they offer a moment of catharsis. I dedicate this book to all those who are heartbroken, troubled, confused and are looking for solace and a little fun. I am indebted to the greats like William Wordsworth, John Milton, Robert Frost, John Donne, Emily Bronte, Francois Villon, Charles Baudelaire, to name a few. For in them, I draw inspiration and attempt to write. I wish this endeavour would prove to be worthy of reading. Please bear with me if there are any shortcomings.

Acknowledgement

This book is, on the one hand, a sum total of all the deceptions I have gone through and, at the same time, all the lessons I have learnt. Sometimes, I feel I am just a mere observer. I am grateful to all the villains as well as the good angels who were part of my life, as they are the reason behind my so-called wisdom. Hence, I thank all of them for being foremost my teachers. On the other hand, this compilation is a result of introspection that happened every day before a good night's sleep.

Preface

A collection of poems, written with the purpose of exploring the human mind. I hope, while reading, they not only amuse us but also enlighten us. The themes chosen revolve around unity with an underlying essence that all are one. There is no difference between you and I, and yet everything begins with I and ends with I in a self-centred world. Where is the space for the other? The other is also equally important because I is also other for the other. In a nutshell, we are all one family.

1. Teenage

In my life, I have done big
Or at least, I thought so
Building memories worth remembering
Yet full of silly bits that flow
Playing Ludo, Snakes and Ladders and
Scrabble
How I grew up into a boy of mettle.

A face innocent and gay
Friends, games, snacks, only matter
Time flew from silver light through blanket
grey
We hardly cared about the hereafter
Children were we to play deceitful
Far away from life's hustle and bustle.

One fine day, caught our eyes piggytails.
Soft, sweet, singing in the rain
Mesmerised, we forgot our tales
We heard the music of the mandolin
Melting our hearts with pure joy
Time ceased for a moment, Oh boy.

Was it the season of Spring
When the flowers bloom
Was it the time of fairies dancing
In the meadows, exhuming perfume
How I grew into a boy of mettle
Far away from life's hustle and bustle.

2. Message

These letters to you I write
I send in them, my heart
Little happiness and wishes
I share with you my desires.

    I feel at ease writing them
    As if my pain is taken away with a
grin
    What then even if I am alone
    You are always in my thoughts aflame.

    Little is distance between us
    When I post them to you thus.
    Each day I wait for your reply
    And when it comes, is a great joy.

These letters to me you write
You send in them, your heart
Little sorrows and glee
We, in them, could share free.

3. Eden

You ask me a simple question and I
tell you a simple answer
    Knowing the unknown has always
been my desire
    Let it be a man or a woman
    Since the beginning, we have been in
sin
    It is that curiosity of Eve
    Which taught mankind to till
    What am I then to obey and be
contended

With the given form, remain
enlightened
         No, each day tricks my heart to taste
         The fruit red in distant least
         Let me relish eating what I want
         And then let me enjoy confronting
what I am not.
         As a man, I always need a companion
         And with her, it is always Eden.
         I, poor creature, know not the
temporalness,
         As, He is yet to show his wrath on us,
         Then it produced many a brook into
an ocean
         So, we multiplied infinite from a
small portion.
         Until evil in disguise of a serpent
came,
         And changeth the beautiful mind of a
poor dame.

4. Hearth

The science behind our fry-pan
Are the dosas made in shape fine,
Not only they are tasty and spicy
But also attract eyes dicy.

Newly bought our pan on flame
Resembles the purity gold claim
The brown tan on its surface
Is smoother than icy ballet space.

I wonder how firm it is made
Surpasses the King, newly crowned
Here, you might think it is an
exaggeration
But I don't want to kill this very
notion.

Suppressing the ideas trivial in your
heart
Can bring inability to express your
heart
For howsoever small the matter may
be
Will leave its mark in your heart
permanently.

Though thinkst me vacillating
With this poem, I am playing
But to grasp the love is your hand
Only the lamp lit will show the
creation grand.

5. Allure

Her face beautiful is my torture
    Her every gesture is my sceptre
    Her each step makes my heart heavy
    As I gazed upon her steady.

    Her eyes beautiful, I praise Him
    Precision achieved in creating them
    As she smiled, I stumbled a little
    And in mist thick, she became
invisible.

    Throughout night, I couldn't sleep
    Because her created wounds were
deep
    There was no such medicine held
    To cure the disease, so called.

Tender age knew not infatuation
Sunken in gloom, wondering our relation
Those fascinating moments and more to come
Realised as hurtful truth due from Him.

6. Jealousy

Thy mind coarse, laughs at my muse
>Unable to comprehend the meaning
sage
>Thy face ugly changing the course
>Clearly, I see how your jealousy
eclipse.

>The blood in my veins ran fast
>As my poor heart shrunk at last
>Covetousness killed the mind healthy
>Your own blood felt sick and filthy.

To myself, I murmured as we
proceeded
        Upside down, the whole world looked
        What is the use of a beautiful nest,
        when the birds could not lay eggs in
it.

7. Wretched Beauty

What sin she committed
To live life so wretched
Sleep in slums gutted
What in life is the gain
To live life so vain.

Hens pecking, cows chewing
nearby, she is washing laundry
Then in spring, she becomes young,
Realising her beauty, melodies she

sang.

Forgetting all the pain, enduring till then
She yearned to transcend the world with a grin
She advanced her coins in Cupid's game
And lost her innocence with shame.

8. Flow with the Nature

I want to run along with day and
night
I want to cloth under the sun
I want to get nude under the stars
But I see everyone busy
And have no time for each other.

I want to drench when it rains
I want to freeze when it is cold
I want to tan when it is hot
But everyone is running after money
So that tomorrow they can enjoy
seasons.

I want to sleep under the trees
I want to drink from the brooks
I want to touch clouds atop the hills
I want to swim in the sea
But where is the time, friends
Are not you nearing the tomb?

I want to cover my body with desert
sand
I want to sit on a camel's hump
I want to roll over sand dunes
I want to see sand storms
But everyone is busy partying.

I want to travel in the forest
I want to see tigers preying
I want to hear serpents hissing
I want to watch animals drinking
water
But everyone is sleepwalking with
mobiles.

I want to see children playing
I want to calm them when they are
crying

I want to offer them ice cream
I want to clad them in colourful
dresses
I want to play with them all day long
But parents are busy fighting their
egos.

Where is the harmony
Where is the joy

Of living with nature, oh family,
Of dining together
Of exchanging words of comfort
After a tiresome day.

Where is the ecstasy
Of sharing the same shelter with a big
family
Where is the comfort of
The tender rays of the sun under
which,
Us, drink tea early morning in the
courtyard.
Where are those cozy evenings
When we assemble in the veranda

And discuss boasting stories
of our little big brothers, our heroes
When suddenly the smell of freshly
cooked porridge, fish fry
And fried pappadums pass through
the front hall.
And we run in, train inside the house
with a roar.

9. Death

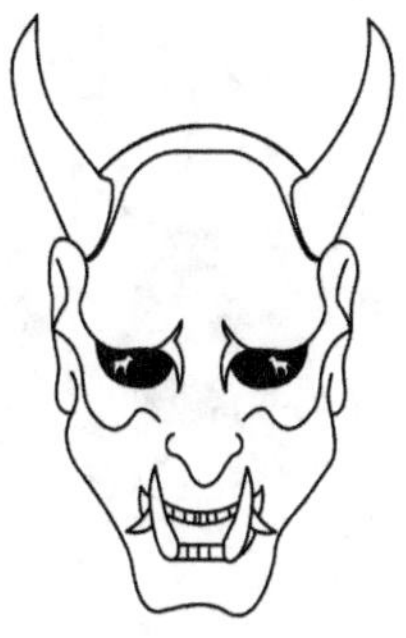

Fear not the death
Fear not the life
Fear the moment
That precipitates life
And puts you to sleep.
That transient second
Is scarier than how
An infant feels minutes after birth.
That cosy cocoon's comfort
From which you are scooped out
To the unfamiliar world
Is not it what one is anxious of.

10. Campus

Ducks are starving and quacking
Youth are giggling and walking
Weather is pleasant
Campus is vibrant
Where else is heaven
If it is not here even.

Fish are desperate for a morsel
Pretty girls with umbrellas hurry
Sky is dark, and cold is the drizzle
Everything looks grey and misty
Where else is heaven
If it is not here even.

11. Farmer

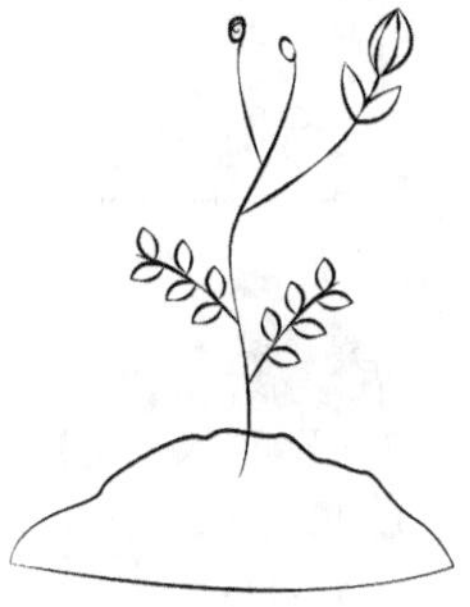

Brisk is the morning
    Risk is in the furlong
    Fields are large
    Work is huge.

    Weather is friendly
    Rain is ready
    For the seeds to sprout
    And transform into a plant.

    Farmers are happy
Wishes will be soon true
    Not many though in the loop
    only to dump the mortgage load.

12. Hanged

Brothers, who live after us,
Do not have hardened hearts against us,
Because if you have pity on us,
God will show mercy on you.
You will see us attached five or six
And to the flesh that we had nourished,
Was left decomposed, consumed and rotten,
And we, the bones, converted into ashes and
powder,
Of our misfortune, let nobody laugh;
But pray to God that all of us are absolved!

If we call you brothers, do not look upon us
With disdain, though we had been killed
By law, however, you must be aware
That not all men have righteous minds;
Forgive us, now that we are no more,
for the son of the Virgin Mary,
That his grace has not vanished,
Saving us from the infernal Fire.
We are dead, should our soul annoy us;
But pray to God that all of us are absolved!

The rain had dissipated and washed us,
And had dried and blackened us;
Magpies and crows had dug out our eyes,
And pulled our beard and eyebrows,
Never were we at rest,
Then this, then that, we had been blown by the wind
Shifting continuously at its will,
More bird-pecking than it could be sewn,
Do not leave us;
But pray to God that all of us are absolved!

Oh Jesus, who is Lord to all,
Save us from the fury of Hell
Let Satan have no claim on us.
Men, never mock at us,
But pray to God that all of us are absolved!

13. Union

When I see you, my heart finds peace,
But a flame deep inside flickers
When I smell you, my mind settles,
But your eyes beckon to forbidden dreams
When you speak, I hear music
But a temptation to lock lips, I cannot desist
When you sit next to me,
Everything under the sky looks happy.

When you touch me, I feel alive
But my thoughts go wild with desire
When you get angry, I see your eyebrows
dance
But I am longing for a kiss
The sweat on your temples reminds

Of dew drops on tender leaves
When I listen to your breath
I forget all my worries
and wish to become one.

14. Hope

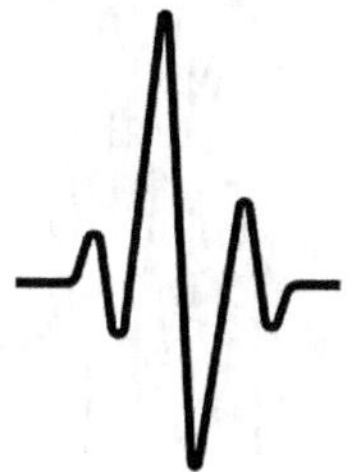

We reach for the sky with dreams
But we often fail as suffer our stars
Like autumn leaves that wither
Lose the height, our hopes and desire
Like winds that howl and whine
Which could have been divine
For in failure, a lesson we learn
And a reason to rise again
Stronger, wiser, as it is not the end
And our hearts leave sadness behind.

15. Victory

With arms raised, we roar
The sweet taste of victory we savour
Our glory shines like a rising sun
That gleams orange over the horizon.

Through struggles and strife, we paved our
way
We stumbled and fell and fought again all day
Victory that seemed far away at the dawn
In a wink, we conquered the enemy
And added another feather to the crown.

16. An Evening of Serenity

A gentle breeze in a quiet place
Faraway from the chaos
A fireplace, a brook nearby
A book to read and a heath to cover by.

Tall pines all over, covered with a fog – grey
A glass of wine stirring my soul
I stare, unaware, at the drizzle
At the entrance, pets on my doormat snuggle.

A perfect evening to sip and reminisce over a
photo album
Songs in the background and romance in the
cerebellum
You recline and nibble hors d'oeuvres
Hearing whispers from distant quarters
On a road that descends to the valley of roses.

17. Pain

Pleasure we can share
But pain is our own
we celebrate happiness
but remain to ourselves in sickness
we moan in pain silently
but have fun pompously
opulent palaces, kings majestic
about whom we read in books of history
extravagant lifestyles and royal evenings
of which we never dreamt of, narrate,
most of them died either in sorrow or disease
so please do not be egoistic
since the secret is unravelled.

18. Care

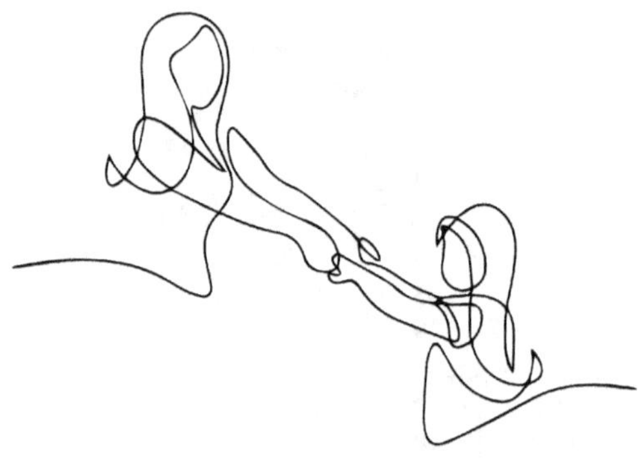

In times of need, we seek a helping hand
A gentle gesture, a tender embrace
A warm hug is what soothes the mind
Of money, a must, I do not impose
Because the poor know from the day of birth
How secure, comfortable it makes life and
attracts mirth
In these acts of care, we heal fast
And each day brightens up with confidence
vast.

19. Madness and Devotion

Between madness and devotion, is there any
difference
One is passion and another is reverence
Both have no boundaries and restrictions
Society may have reservations
But love is the emotion that dominates

Madness has no direction; devotion has
reason
Madness may turn into insanity
It descends into obscurity
Into darkness and confusion
From where there is no point of return

Devotion on the other hand illuminates
It is a nest of creative pursuits
Many a poet wrote maxims
Upon them, humanity relies.

It is a source of inspiration
It is a product of perspiration
Of body and soul, together they create
An embodiment of truth and precept.

20. Innocence

Child is a face of innocence
Innocence is an essence of godliness
Innocence is immaculate, honest heart
As pure as the inside of coconut.

Innocence charms us with gentle might
Filling our lives with virtuous delight
It is a gift marvellous from heaven
to humanity as to teach a lesson.

For we forgot in our busy schedule
To appreciate modesty and things of virtue
Angels surround children of paradise
Unto them, we bow with gratitude.

21. Ego

Ego, like a shadow, follows us
It is a constant voice that is restless
When it takes control, there is no remorse
You challenge God with pride

Forgotten from where you come
Jumping agog with false prestige
Surrounded by idiots and sycophants
Not realising how much life is transient

God will give a befitting answer
As he keeps watch from above
His patience is great and he is tolerant
But do not test them, as damnation will not
wait.